NEW 9-1 G REVISIO.. ... FOR WILLIAM SHAKESPEARE'S *THE MERCHANT OF VENICE* - Study guide (Page-by-page analysis)

by Joe Broadfoot

All rights reserved

Copyright © Joe Broadfoot, 2016

The right of Joe Broadfoot to be identified as the author of this work has been asserted in accordance with Section 77 of the Copyright, Designs and Patents Act 1988

**ISBN-13:
978-1539885467**

**ISBN-10:
1539885461**

9-1 GCSE REVISION NOTES – The Merchant of Venice

CONTENTS

Introduction 3
Best essay practice 4
Essay planning 5
New specification 8
Basic plot - ACTIVITY 13
ACTIVITY answers 15
Context 17
Act One 20
Act Two 27
Act Three 33
Act Four 38
Act Five 42
Sample Essay Question and Guidance Notes 44
Characters 56
Essay writing tips 59
Glossary 64

Brief Introduction

This book is aimed at GCSE students of English Literature who are studying William Shakespeare's *The Merchant of Venice*. The focus is on what examiners are looking for, especially since the changes to the curriculum in 2015, and here you will find each scene covered in detail. I hope this will help you and be a valuable tool in your studies and revision.

Criteria for high marks

Make sure you use appropriate critical language (see glossary of literary terms at the back). You need your argument to be fluent, well-structured and coherent. Stay focused!

Analyse and explore the use of form, structure and the language. Explore how these aspects affect the meaning.

Make connections between texts and look at different interpretations. Explore their strengths and weaknesses. Don't forget to use supporting references to strengthen your argument.

Analyse and explore the context.

Best essay practice

9-1 GCSE REVISION NOTES – The Merchant of Venice

There are so many way to write an essay. Although exam boards discourage formulas, many schools use **PEE** for paragraphs: point/evidence/explain. Others use **PETER**: point/evidence/technique/explain/reader; **PEEL**: point, example, explain, link; **PEEE**: point/evidence/explain/explore. Whichever method you use, make sure you mention the **writer's effects**. This generally is what most students forget to add. You must think of what the writer is trying to achieve by using a particular technique and what is actually achieved. Do not just spot techniques and note them. You may get some credit for using appropriate technology, but unless you can comment on the effect created on the reader and/or the writer's intention, you will miss out on most of the marks available.

Essay planning

In order to write a good essay it is necessary to plan. In fact, it is best to quite formulaic in an exam situation, as you won't have much time to get started. Therefore I will ask you to learn the following acronym: **DATMC (Definition, Application, Terminology, Main, Conclusion**. Some schools call it: **GSLMC (General, Specific, Link, Main, Conclusion)**, but it amounts to the same thing. The first three letters concern the introduction. (Of course, the alternative is to leave some blank lines and write your introduction after you have completed the main body of your essay, but it is probably not advisable for most students).

Let us first look at the following exam question, which is on poetry (of course, the same essay-planning principles apply to essays on novels and plays as well).

QUESTION: Explore how the poet conveys **feelings** in the poem.

STEP ONE: Identify the **keyword** in the question. (I have already done this, by highlighting it in **bold**). If you are following GSLMC, you now need to make a **general statement** about what feelings are. Alternatively, if you're following DATMC, simply **define** 'feelings'. For example, 'Feelings are emotion states or reactions or vague, irrationals ideas and beliefs'.

STEP TWO: If you are following GSLMC, you now need to make a **specific statement** linking feelings (or whatever else you've defined) to how they appear in the poem. Alternatively, if you're following DATMC, simply define which

9-1 GCSE REVISION NOTES – The Merchant of Venice

'feelings' **apply** in this poem. For example, 'The feelings love, fear and guilt appear in this poem, and are expressed by the speaker in varying degrees.'

STEP THREE: If you are following GSLMC, you now need to make a **link statement** identifying the methods used to convey the feelings (or whatever else you've defined) in the poem. Alternatively, if you're following DATMC, simply define which **techniques** are used to convey 'feelings' in this poem. For example, 'The poet primarily uses alliteration to emphasise his heightened emotional state, while hyperbole and enjambment also help to convey the sense that the speaker is descending into a state of madness.

STEP FOUR: Whether you are following GSLMC or DATMC, the next stage is more or less the same. The main part of the essay involves writing around **six paragraphs**, using whichever variation of PEEE you prefer. In my example, I will use **Point, Evidence, Exploration, Effect** on the listener. To make your essay even stronger, try to use your quotations chronologically. It will be easier for the examiner to follow, which means you are more likely to achieve a higher grade. To be more specific, I recommend that you take and analyse two quotations from the beginning of the poem, two from the middle, and two at the end.

STEP FIVE: Using Carol Ann Duffy's poem, 'Stealing', here's an example of how you could word one of your six paragraphs: **(POINT)** 'Near the beginning of the poem, the speaker's determination is expressed.' **(EVIDENCE)** 'This is achieved through the words: 'Better off dead than giving in'. **(EXPLORATION)**. The use of 'dead' emphasizes how far the speaker is prepared to go in pursuit of what he wants, although there is a sense that he is exaggerating (hyperbole). **(EFFECT)** The listener senses that the speaker may be immature given how prone he is to exaggerate his own bravery.

STEP SIX: After writing five or more paragraphs like the one above, it will be time to write a **conclusion**. In order to do that, it is necessary to sum up your previous points and evaluate them. This is not the time to introduce additional quotations. Here is an example of what I mean: 'To conclude, the poet clearly conveys the speaker's anger. Although the listener will be reluctant to completely sympathise with a thief, there is a sense that the speaker is suffering mentally, which makes him an interesting and partially a sympathetic character. By using a dramatic monologue form, the poet effectively conveys the speaker's mental anguish, which makes it easier to more deeply understand what first appears to be inexplicable acts of violence.

Other tips

Make your studies active!

Don't just sit there reading! Never forget to annotate, annotate and annotate!

9-1 GCSE REVISION NOTES – The Merchant of Venice

All line references refer to the 2016 sixth edition of *The Merchant of Venice* published by Cambridge University Press (ISBN-978-1-107-61539-7).

The Merchant of Venice

AQA (New specification starting in 2015)

If you're studying for an AQA qualification in English Literature, there's a good chance your teachers will choose this text to study. There are good reasons for that: it's moralistic and familiar to students. The text encourages us to think about right and wrong.

However, one of the difficulties is the language. That can't be helped, bearing in mind that part A of the exam paper involves answering questions on Shakespeare, whereas part B is all about the 19th-century novel.

To further complicate things, the education system is in a state of flux: that means we have to be ready for constant change. Of course, everyone had got used to grades A,B and C meaning a pass. It was simple, it was straightforward and nearly everyone understood it. Please be prepared that from this day henceforward, the top grade will now be known as 9. Grade 4 will be the equivalent of a C grade, although the government want students to aim for a good pass, or a low B, which will be grade 5.

Now onto the exam itself. As I said, paper 1 consists of Shakespeare and the 19th-century novel. It is a written closed book exam (in other words you are not allowed to have the texts with you), which lasts one hour 45 minutes. You can score 64 marks, which amounts to 40% of your GCSE grade. The other 60% is gained from paper 2, which is all about modern texts, poetry and unseen poetry. But enough about paper 2, as our concern here is paper 1 and more specifically section A: Shakespeare.

In section B, students will be expected to write in detail about an extract from the novel they have studied in class and then write about the novel as a whole. Just for the record, the choices of novel are the following: *The Strange Case of Dr Jekyll and Mr Hyde* by Robert Louis Stevenson, *A Christmas Carol* and *Great Expectations* by Charles Dickens, *Jane Eyre* by Charlotte Brontë, *Frankenstein* by Mary Shelley, *Pride and Prejudice* by Jane Austin, and The Sign of Four by Sir Arthur Conan Doyle.

Another important thing to consider is the fact that for section B of paper 1, you will not be assessed on assessment objective 4 (AO4), which involves spelling, punctuation, grammar and vocabulary. This will be assessed on section A of paper 1, which is about Shakespeare, and it will be worth 2.5% of your overall GCSE grade. In terms of raw marks, it is worth 4 out of 64. So for once, we need not concern ourselves with what is affectionately known as 'SPAG' too much.

However, it is necessary to use the correct literary terminology wherever possible to make sure we maximise our marks on assessment objective2 (AO2). AO2 tests how well we can analyse language form and structure. Additionally, we

9-1 GCSE REVISION NOTES – The Merchant of Venice

are expected to state the effect the writer tried to create and how it impacts on the reader.

This brings me onto assessment objective 1 (AO1), which involves you writing a personal response to the text. It is important that you use quotations to backup your points of view. Like AO2, AO1 is worth 15% of your GCSE on Paper 1.

Assessment objective 3 (AO3) is worth half of that, but nevertheless it is important to comment on context to make sure you get as much of the 7.5% up for grabs as you can.

So just to make myself clear, there are 30 marks available in section B for your answer on the 19th-century novel. Breaking it down even further, you will get 12 marks maximum the backing up your personal opinion with quotations, an additional 12 marks for analysing the writer's choice of words for effect (not forgetting to use appropriate terminology - more on that see the glossary at the back of this book), and six marks for discussing context.

As you can see, we've got a lot to get through so without further ado let's get on with the actual text itself and possible exam questions.

Previous exam questions

Notwithstanding the governmental changes to the grading system, it is still good practice to go over previous exam papers. I'm looking at a specimen paper, which asks students to read an extract from Act 1 Scene 3, which begins: Signior Antonio, many a time and oft / In the Rialto you have rated me' (p25). It ends with: 'You called me dog: and for these courtesies I'll lend you thus much monies.'(p25).

Students are expected to read the extract and comment about how Shakespeare presents Shylock's feelings about how he's treated. Students should say how that is shown in the extract itself and also on the whole novel. Despite the changes to the syllabus which have made GCSEs more difficult to pass, future questions are likely to be very similar. Of course, it could be about a different character, but it will involve looking at the extract for the first part of the question and then moving on to discuss the whole novel. That's the format and is unlikely to change in the near future. So no worries there then!

To make sure that you meet AQA's learning objectives and get a high mark, make sure you go into the exam knowing something about the following:

- the plot
- the characters
- the theme

9-1 GCSE REVISION NOTES – The Merchant of Venice

- selected quotations/details
- exam skills

Now, we will be going through each of those objectives in turn, so you should be well prepared for the exam itself.

Basic plot – ACTIVITY (Spoiler alert!)

Okay, let's not have any silly jokes about losing the plot; instead let me ask you to rearrange these events (scenes) in *The Merchant of Venice.* You should be able to try it even if you haven't read the text yet. It will help you think about the dramatic structure of the play.

Event A: Jessica prepares to run away from home.

Event B: Antonio and Bassanio discuss Portia.

Event C: Lorenzo hears Shylock will be away from home.

Event D: Portia and Nerissa discuss suitors.

Event E: Shylock leaves for the feast.

Event F: Shylock and Antonio agree 'the bond'.

Event G: Jessica elopes with Lorenzo.

Event H: Portia meets Morocco.

Event I: Morocco chooses a casket.

Event J: Lancelot leaves Shylock to join Bassanio.

Event K: One of Antonio's ships is lost at sea.

Event L: Shylock hears of Antonio's losses.

Event M: The husbands admit their indiscretions.

Event N: The trial.

9-1 GCSE REVISION NOTES – The Merchant of Venice

Event O: The wives test their husbands.

Event P: Jessica reveals she is now a Christian.

Event Q: Antonio is imprisoned.

Event R: Portia plans to rescue Antonio.

Event S: Arragon chooses a casket.

Event T: Bassanio chooses a casket.

ANSWERS

Now let's make sure that you got that in the right order. Here is the **correct sequence** of events (Act number and scene number is in brackets):

Event B: Antonio and Bassanio discuss Portia. (1.1)

Event D: Portia and Nerissa discuss suitors. (1.2)

Event F: Shylock and Antonio agree 'the bond'. (1.3)

Event H: Portia meets Morocco. (2.1)

Event J: Lancelot leaves Shylock to join Bassanio. (2.2)

Event A: Jessica prepares to run away from home. (2.3)

Event C: Lorenzo hears Shylock will be away from home. (2.4)

Event E: Shylock leaves for the feast. (2.5)

Event G: Jessica elopes with Lorenzo. (2.6)

Event I: Morocco chooses a casket. (2.7)

Event K: One of Antonio's ships is lost at sea. (2.8)

Event S: Arragon chooses a casket. (2.9)

Event L: Shylock hears of Antonio's losses. (3.1)

Event T: Bassanio chooses a casket. (3.2)

Event Q: Antonio is imprisoned. (3.3)

9-1 GCSE REVISION NOTES – The Merchant of Venice

Event R: Portia plans to rescue Antonio. (3.4)

Event P: Jessica reveals she is now a Christian. (3.5)

Event N: The trial. (4.1)

Event O: The wives test their husbands. (4.2)

Event M: The husbands admit their indiscretions. (5.1)

How many did you get right? Even if you get all of them right, try again later.

CONTEXT

Although mentioning context is not as important as language analysis and responding to the question, it is, nevertheless, a good starting point. If you can understand some of the reasons why Shakespeare may have written the way he did, it should enhance your understanding of the text.

Although dates are not exact, the years when *The Merchant of Venice* was written was between 1596 and 1598. The reigning monarch at the time was the ageing, unmarried and childless Elizabeth I, who had been on the throne for forty years, during which time Protestantism was the official religion.

Unsurprisingly, religion is an important theme that you will encounter in the play. You must also remember that Shakespeare performed and wrote plays for the Queen, as a member of the Lord Chamberlain's Men. As the name suggests, all the actors were men during Shakespeare's time, so when female characters cross-dressed, they were, in fact, reverting back to their original gender! Of course, that aspect is lost in most modern productions of Shakespearean plays, which tend to have a unisex cast.

In fact, it is not unusual for Shakespeare's plays to have cross-dressing female characters. *The Two Gentlemen of Verona* (1594), *As You Like It* (1600) and *Twelfth Night* (1600) are three comedies that employ this plot device. However, there is much debate about whether or not *The Merchant of Venice*

9-1 GCSE REVISION NOTES – The Merchant of Venice

is a comedy. Due to the tragic elements in it, the play is often described as a tragicomedy.

However, from a contextual point of view, we could say that Shakespeare was deliberately empowering females, particularly at a time when the monarch was female. Like Elizabeth I, cross-dressing women in Shakespearean plays are portrayed as active, determined and intelligent.

Now let's consider the settings: Venice was considered to be a stylish place, whereas Belmont is fictional. This implies that there is tension between the male-dominated, public practicalities of money and the female-dominated, private fantasy world of romance. The differences between England and Venice was marked and perhaps the most relevant aspect to remark upon was that the Italian city-state was more international and had a large number of Jews living there. By contrast, three hundred years before Shakespeare's time, Jews had been officially banished from England. However, a couple of years before the play was performed, a Jewish doctor named Roderigo Lopez was executed for allegedly attempting to poison the Queen.

Even before this event, it was already common to blame Jews for all manner of afflictions, even the plague. They were an easy target to attack, as before their banishment, some had accumulated a lot of wealth from money-lending. Perhaps because of the official Christian position on charging interest, the word 'Jew' had become a term of verbal abuse for money-lenders, who were less than generous with their terms for repayment. In Elizabethan England, the legal amount of interest on a loan had to be ten percent or less, whereas in rich Venice, the amount to repay could be more than double or quadruple that interest rate. Therefore, to Elizabethans, all loans repayable with interest in Venice would have been considered usurious and sinful.

The original source of Shakespeare's play is thought to be a story called: 'Il Pecorone', which means 'blockhead'. It is about a young man called Gianetto, who attempts to woo the Widow of Belmont, using money borrowed from his friend, Ansaldo. As in Shakerspeare's play, Ansaldo has to use a Jewish money-lender to finance Gianetto. Other similarities include the 'pound of flesh' bond and a cross-dressing lawyer.

9-1 GCSE REVISION NOTES – The Merchant of Venice

Act 1 Scene 1

The scene begins with Antonio bemoaning the fact that he doesn't know why he's so sad: 'I know not why I am so sad' (1). He admits that he doesn't understand himself: 'I must not understand myself very well' (7). We know he is melancholy, but we don't know why. It feels as if the play has begun in mid-conversation, or if it were a novel it would be described as in media res.

Salarino claims that Antonio's 'mind is tossing on the ocean', which alludes to his merchant ships at sea (8). Salarino seems to admire Antonio and his business enterprise, as, using a simile, he compares the ships to 'signors and rich burghers' (10).

Solanio, meanwhile, appears to mildly rebuke Antonio for not being content. If he were in Antonio's shoe, he would be 'plucking the grass' to find out the wind's direction (18). In other words, he would be too busy to be worried.

By contrast, Salarino seems more respectful and understanding. He can easily imagine how Antonio's worries about 'his merchandise' might cause him anxiety (40).

However, Antonio denies that his merchant ships are the cause of his sadness. He admits he is hedging his bets, as his merchandise is not all in 'one bottom trusted' (42). He also denies that he is 'in love', when Solanio suggests that (46-7).

Solanio mentioned 'two-headed Janus', a Roman god, who is linked with the villainous Iago from Othello, which was written around a decade later (50). Perhaps Solanio is suggesting that Antonio is being two-faced in not revealing what is bothering him. He compares the condition to those who refuse to laugh even if a joke is declared hilarious by 'Nestor', a Greek king who was renowned for his seriousness (56).

As soon as Bassanio arrives, Solanio tells Antonio that they will leave him 'with better company' (59). It seems as if he's being ironic, as Solarino adds that he would have stayed had 'worthier friends...not prevented' him (61).

Bassanio notes that Solanio and Salarino are growing 'exceedingly strange' as they leave (67). Salarino's parting words: 'We'll make our leisures to attend on yours' suggests there is no bad blood between them. Perhaps it is the presence of Lorenzo or Gratiano that has caused Solanio and Salarino to leave.

Gratiano immediately points out that Antonio looks 'not well' (73). He interrupts Antonio midline and through stichomythia the idea that Gratiano is verbally dominant is effectively conveyed. Gratiano insists on playing 'The Fool', and a Shakespearean audience would expect such a character to speak the truth albeit in a comedic way (79).

Gratiano insists that silence is not necessarily golden or wise,

9-1 GCSE REVISION NOTES – The Merchant of Venice

which allows Lorenzo to state that he 'must be one of these same dumb wise men' as the former never lets him speak (106).

Lorenzo and Gratiano exit, which allows Bassanio to talk to Antonio privately about the former's 'secret pilgrimage' to a love interest (119).

Bassanio reveals that 'her name is Portia' (164). He ranks her as highly 'Cato's daughter, Brutus' Portia' (165). This allusion to the wife of one of Julius Caesar's assassins does not seem to augur well. Neither does the reference to how 'her sunny locks/Hang on her temples like a golden fleece' (168-9). Jason may have won the fleece and a wife called Medea, but in the myth his wife kills his children, so the comparison appears to be unflattering.

Bassanio appears to be foolish and over-confident, as he asserts: 'I should question less be fortunate' (175). Antonio promises to enquiry 'where money is' to help finance Bassanio's quest to gain the hand of Portia (184).

Act 1 Scene 2

The scene changes from Venice to Belmont, the garden of Portia's house. Like Antonio, Portia is bemoaning her predicament. Unlike Antonio, instead of sad, she is 'aweary of this great world' (1). It seems like another version of ennui.

Nerissa seems to warning Portia not to be so self-indulgent, saying 'competency lives longer' than 'superfluity' (8-9, 8). We wonder if she's being a little sycophantic, as she panders to Portia a little by saying that to 'starve with nothing' is on a par with having 'too much' (5-6, 5).

Portia finds some wisdom in those comments and realises that her problem is psychological. She admits that 'poor men's cottages' can become 'princes' palaces' if people perceive them to be thus (12). The plosive 'p' in these alliterative lines seem borne of frustration. She is honest enough to realise it's difficult to practise what you preach or 'follow' your 'own teaching' (15). The nub of her problem is that her 'will' has been 'curbed by the will of a dead father' (21). The repetition of 'will' implies she has plenty of will-power, but is powerless in this situation.

Nerissa seems a little pessimistic about Portia's chances of finding true love as she says: 'The lottery that he hath devised...will no doubt never be chosen by any rightly' (24-27). This foreshadows the idea that Portia must help her favourite suitor to succeed.

Nerissa asks about the Neapolitan prince, to which Portia bawdily replies: 'I am much afeared my lady that his mother played false with a smith' (36-7). Portia is suggesting that he was born out of wedlock and loves horses because his real father was a blacksmith. The sexual and lewd content in her speeches here make prose more appropriate than verse.

9-1 GCSE REVISION NOTES – The Merchant of Venice

Portia complains about her other suitors: the County Palatine does 'nothing but frown' (39); the copycat, Monsieur Le Bon 'is every man in no man' (49); the poor linguist, Falconbridge 'hath neither Latin, French, nor Italian' but has boxed 'the ear' of the Scottish lord (57, 65); while the drunkard Duke of Saxony's nephew is likened to 'a sponge' (81). Unsurprisingly, Portia thinks she 'will die as chaste as Diana', the Roman goddess of virginity, even if she lives to be as old as the Greek prophetess, Sibylla (87). These comments would have been well received by the reigning monarch at the time, Elizabeth I, who remained unmarried, but like Portia was inundated with suitors.

Portia unconvincingly pretends she cannot remember 'a Venetian, a scholar and a soldier' (92-3). However, initially, her enthusiasm gets the better of her, as she replies to Nerissa's enquiry: 'Yes, yes, it was Bassanio! - as I think so was he called'.

Her reaction to Bassanio is in stark contrast to her comment about the latest suitor: the Prince of Morocco. Portia would rather he 'shrive' than 'wive' her, with the rhyme emphasising how unpalatable it would be to marry someone with 'the complexion of the devil' (108, 107). These views reflect Elizabethan ideas about the beauty of skin colour, as it was not uncommon for women to apply lead to their skins to make themselves whiter and therefore more beautiful, in their eyes.

Act 1 Scene 3

The scene reverts to Venice and again we appear to be in mid-conversation as Shylock ponders Bassanio's request. Shylock continually repeats the word 'well' and the request for 'three thousand ducats for three months' (1, 3, 5, 8). It's almost as if Shylock cannot believe his good fortune to have Antonio 'bound' for this loan (9).

Perhaps because of the base nature of money-lending, their conversation is in prose. Shylock believes that Antonio may struggle to pay the sum back as 'his means are in supposition' (14-15).

Although he is keen to seal a deal, Shylock refuses to 'eat...drink' or 'pray' with Bassanio and Antonio for religious reasons (30). Shylock's mention of Jesus Christ conjuring 'the devil' by allowing Christians to eat pork would not have been well received by an Elizabethan audience (28).

Shylock's aside shortly afterwards allows him to confide with the audience, but Elizabethans may have offended by his reasons for hating Antonio 'for he is a Christian' (34). However, they may have been amused by his comments about Antonio looking 'like a fawning publican' or taxman, as that would play to the stereotype of Jews hating to part with money (33). Audiences may have seen Shylock as the stereotypical villain they would love to hate.

Despite being a stereotypical money-grabber, Shylock is not

9-1 GCSE REVISION NOTES – The Merchant of Venice

selfish. He thinks of his religion and the implications of forgiving Antonio when he says: 'Cursed be my tribe if I forgive him!' (42-43).

Since Antonio's entry, the language has switched from prose to verse, which suggests that the subject matter is more lofty than money-lending. However, Shylock links religion with profit when he says: 'thrift is blessing' while commenting on the Biblical story of Jacob from the Old Testament (82).

Antonio seems unimpressed by Shylock's Biblical references as he says: 'the devil can cite Scripture for his purpose' (90). Clearly, Antonio doesn't trust Shylock, but he is over-confident enough to underestimate him, perhaps.

The audience may begin to sympathise more with Shylock, as he mentions how Antonio has spat upon his 'Jewish gaberdine' and has voided his 'rheum upon' his 'bears' (104, 109). These graphic descriptions are not denied by Antonio, so it casts the latter into a less than flattering light.

Antonio shows no remorse and says that he is 'like to call' Shylock a dog 'again' (122). This shows how deep prejudice runs in Venetian society.

When the harsh terms of the bond are divulged, Bassanio honourably says to Antonio: 'You shall not seal to such a bond for me' (147). However, Antonio is guilty of over-confidence as he says: 'I will not forfeit it' (149).

Antonio continues in this overconfident vein, foreshadowing the future with a Gentile pun, calling Shylock 'the gentle Jew', who 'will turn Christian' (170, 171).

Act 2 Scene 1

The Prince of Morocco asks Portia to see past his 'complexion' and he uses the semantic field of war to convince her of his qualities. He calls his skin colour the 'shadowed livery' or uniform 'of the burnished sun' and brags that he can terrify the brave or 'valiant' (1, 2, 9).

Using stichomythia, Shakespeare implies Morocco's dominance over Portia and his unwillingness to listen to her. She may be ironic when she says he stands 'as fair/As any comer', but Morocco is too insensitive to pick up any nuances in her speech (20-21).

Morocco continues to brag in his war-like way of his exploits and his 'scimitar' which 'slew the Sophy and a Persian prince' (24-25). The sword may be a phallic symbol, showing that his love for her is more lust than deeply meaningful.

His vanity seems to know no bounds, as he sees himself as possessing Herculean strength, judging by his references to 'Hercules' and 'Alcides' (32, 35). However, even Morocco realises that 'blind Fortune' will dictate his future (36).

The scene ends with religious imagery, as Portia invites him 'to the temple' and he accepts that he will be 'blest - or cursed'st' (43, 46).

Act 1 Scene 2

Lancelot speaks in prose and reveals that he has two sides to his character: 'the fiend' and his 'conscience' (8, 10). This suggests that he may be untrustworthy.

Like Morocco, Lancelot acknowledges the power of Fortune, as he mentions 'fates and destinies' and 'the sisters three' in his speech to his father (50, 51).

He reveals his violent thoughts towards his former master, Shylock, when he says: 'Give him a halter!' (86). He reasons that he is 'famished' and is a 'Jew' himself, if he remains in Shylock's service (87, 91).

Like his father, Gobbo, Lancelot is prone to comic malapropisms, when he tells Bassanio that his 'suit is impertinent' rather than pertinent (113). In a sense, he is wooing Bassanio, who speaks in verse to show his superiority, as he wants to serve him rather than Shylock.

Lancelot acknowledges the power of 'Fortune' by personifying it as 'a good wench' (138, 139). This bawdy language is typical of the character.

Shortly after the clown's exit, Gratiano, the fool, enters. Bassanio describes the latter as 'too wild, too rude, and bold of voice' (152). It is almost as if the truth is frowned upon by those of a more romantic bent.

Gratiano uses the semantic field of religion to show him that he will be on his best behaviour should he go with him to Belmont. He mentions 'a sober habit', 'grace' and 'amen' to signal his intentions to be more respectful than usual (161, 164, 165).

Act 2 Scene 3

Jessica likens Lancelot to her father by calling him 'a merry devil' (2). This shows that he indeed becoming like Shylock by remaining employed by him. The audience can understand why she also wants to leave 'hell' (2).

Her guilt is obvious, though, as she recognises it is a 'heinous sin' to be 'ashamed to be' her 'father's child' (15, 16).

Act 2 Scene 4

Lorenzo asks Lancelot to tell 'gentle Jessica' that he will 'not fail her' (19, 20). Lorenzo uses alliteration and a pun on the word 'Gentile' to remind the audience that Jessica will have to change her religion to marry a Christian.

Whether or not it is genuine love is a moot point, as Lorenzo mentions the 'gold and jewels' that 'she is furnished with' (31). Nevertheless, he uses light imagery to describe her at the end of the scene, when he says: 'Fair Jessica shall be my torchbearer' (39). However, rather than romantic, it could be deemed as practical, as she will actually have to hold aloft the torch as they make off in the night.

Act 2 Scene 5

Shylock's descriptive triplet sounds decidedly unromantic, as he mentions that Jessica may 'sleep, and snore, and rend apparel out' (5). Before that, he suggests she has a tendency to 'gourmandise or over-eat (3). This is either making Shylock sound mean, in that he resents his daughter eating so much which is costly, or it means she does actually eat too much.

Shylock warns her of succumbing to the 'shallow foppery' of the masque, which is ironic as she is about to do just that (34). Wearing a disguise, she is about to abscond or elope with Lorenzo.

Shylock's low opinion of Lancelot is evident, as he describes him as 'snail-slow', sleepier 'than the wildcat' and lazier than 'drones' who 'hive not' (45, 46). This implies that Shylock is an abusive employer.

Act 2 Scene 6

Gratiano uses bawdy language and nautical imagery to emphasise how more pleasure is gained from chasing love than gaining love. The 'strumpet wind' is blamed for causing wrecks, which intertwines the themes of love and money (17,

20).

When Jessica joins Lorenzo, she seems dismayed that she must indeed be the 'torchbearer' and 'hold a candle' to her 'shames' (41, 42). The light imagery seems to backfire on her, showing her in a boy's disguise and a less than romantic light.

However, Lorenzo calls her 'wise, fair and true', a triplet which suggests that he values her (57). Nevertheless, the mild oath he takes previously: 'Beshrew me' suggests that he thinks he may be the victim of a nagging wife if the marriage goes ahead as planned.

Act 2 Scene 7

Back in Belmont, Morocco is about to make his choice from 'several caskets', although there are only three (2). Perhaps, Portia is trying to exaggerate the task ahead to put Morocco off.

Morocco uses sea imagery to convey the idea that suitors have come from miles around to try their luck with Portia. He says: 'they come/As o'er a brook to see fair Portia' (46-47). He makes it sound like it is not really a huge ordeal to travel so far for such a beauty. Once again, the themes of fortune, riches and love are intertwined.

One of the most famously misquoted lines in Shakespeare appears inside the golden casket, as Morocco reads: 'All that glisters is not gold' (65). The alliteration emphasises how foolish he has been in making this choice.

Act 2 Scene 8

Back in Venice, Solanio describes Shylock as a 'dog', who is just as concerned with his lost 'ducats' as he is his 'daughter' (14, 15). Like Salarino, Solanio has no sympathy for Shylock and both ridicule his plight.

Solanio seems to lack sympathy for Antonio also, as he sees his sadness as self-indulgent, judging by his comment that they should relieve him of 'his embraced heaviness' (53).

Act 2 Scene 9

Returning to Belmont, we see the next suitor try his luck. Portia seems to give the Prince of Arragon a clue as she reminds him of the conditions of undertaking the task 'to hazard' for her 'worthless self' (17). The lead casket has the word 'hazard' on the inscription and lead is the least valuable of the three and therefore is the most 'worthless'.

Arragon uses a rhetorical question to emphasise his disappointment at choosing the wrong casket when he says: 'Did I deserve no more than a fool's head?' (58) At least he recognises that he already possessed 'one fool's head' when he 'came to woo', so the audience may have some sympathy for him (74).

Portia's comment that 'the candle singed the moth' reminds the audience that love is a dangerous game and a double-edged sword (78).

Meanwhile, Nerissa acknowledges that 'destiny' is the main reason why suitors fail rather than the 'wisdom' and 'wit' mentioned by Portia, which is not helping suitors to make the right choice (82, 80).

Act 3 Scene 1

Solanio begins by asking Salarino about the latest news from 'the Rialto', Venice's financial district (1). This makes Salarino seem more of a businessman or more knowledgeable of the two.

Salarino then has the opportunity to relay the news in prose that 'Antonio hath a ship of rich lading wrecked' (2-3).

Solanio's reaction is to describe Antonio as 'good' and 'honest', which makes the audience sympathise more with his losses at sea.

Shylock then enters, bemoaning his daughter's 'flight' (21). Salarino admits he knows 'the tailor' who 'made the wings' or her disguise, which allowed her to escape (22-23). Solanio comments that the 'bird was fledged', so Shylock should have expected nothing less. Bird imagery makes Jessica's actions appear natural, lessening any sympathy we may have for Shylock.

9-1 GCSE REVISION NOTES – The Merchant of Venice

The Jew's anger is apparent in the repetition of the phrase 'Let him look to his bond' (37, 38, 39). It is almost as if he blames Antonio for what his daughter had done and now he want to take his vengeance out on him. It makes Shylock appear to be unreasonable.

Shylock reacts even more angrily to Salarino's rhetorical question about taking Antonio's 'flesh': 'What's the good for?' Shylock's response is full of rhetorical questions, including: 'Hath not a Jew eyes?' (46). This speech makes the audience question the racist way that Shylock has been treated and makes him appear to be the product of a deeply unfair and prejudiced society.

Tubal, another Jew, arrives to tell Shylock that he 'cannot find' Jessica (65). Although this makes the audience sympathise with Shylock, as he clearly has sent out friends to look for her in vain, his mercenary response makes him appear hard-hearted and callous. He wishes her dead with 'the jewels in her ear' and 'the ducats in her coffin' (70-71).

Nevertheless, it seems that Jessica has no sense of value, as she has traded 'a ring' for 'a monkey' (93, 94). Rings are very important in the play, as they symbolise loyalty amongst other things. Jessica regards the 'turquoise' ring she has been given by her father, which in turn was given to him by 'Leah', presumably his wife, as little more than a trinket (95-6, 96). She clearly does not appreciate what her father has done for her by bringing her up, which makes us think that either she's ungrateful or that Shylock is an abusive character, who has pushed her over the edge.

Act 3 Scene 2

We return to Belmont, where Portia is advising Bassanio to take his time. Although she says: 'a maiden has no tongue but thought', her advice is lengthy so contradicts her view that women should be seen and not heard (8). She even uses the phrase: 'Beshrew your eyes' that reminds the audience that she could easily become a shrew or nagging wife once she is married (14).

Bassanio tells her that waiting makes him feel in a torturous position, which he metaphorically likens to living 'upon the rack', a common form of Elizabethan torture for disloyalty to the Queen (25). The mythological reference to 'the virgin tribute paid by howling Troy' would have been well received by the reigning monarch, who was also unmarried and seemed surrounded by Herculean-type men hoping to win her favours (56).

While Bassanio prepares himself for the casket task, music plays with the lyrics warning against being taken in by 'fancy' personified or superficial appearances (63). This clues clearly leads Bassanio away from choosing gold or silver.

Bassanio absorbs the content of the message, decrying those that have 'the beards of Hercules' but 'livers as white as milk'

(85, 86). We assume he is genuine and made of sterner stuff based on his comment.

It is easy for Bassanio to reject 'gaudy gold', as he remarks that it was 'hard food for Midas', the mythological king who regretted having the power to turn everything he touched to gold (101, 102).

Keeping in line with Elizabethan notions of beauty, which involved applying lead to the face to keep it white, he is moved by 'paleness' to choose the lead casket (106). Unsurprisingly, as the audience already know that gold and silver are the wrong choices, he finds 'fair Portia's counterfeit' or picture inside, which implies that the whole process of choosing has been unfair (115).

Portia's response to his success is modest, as she describes herself as 'an unlessoned girl', who 'may learn' and 'can learn' (159, 161, 162). Her humility is emphasised by her commitment 'to be directed' by Bassanio (164).

However, she invests a lot of importance in the ring she gives him, warning him that it will 'presage the ruin' of his love should he lose it (173). This brings home the enormity of what Jessica has done previously and will add tension later in the plot.

Gratiano's parallel courting of Nerissa makes the whole courtship process seem superficial, even more so as the couples appear ready to race against each other to have 'the first boy' (213). Bawdy innuendos about 'stake down' add to the feeling that Gratiano and Nerissa's relationship, at least, is far from serious.

However, Gratiano see himself as like Bassanio when he says: 'We are the Jasons, we have won the fleece' (240). That self-congratulatory tone is contrasted with the somber news that follows as Salerio reveals that Shylock is insisting on his pound of flesh from Antonio. The triplet emphasises the enormity of his 'envious plea of forfeiture, of justice, and his bond' (282).

Portia declares that she and Nerissa 'will live as maids and widows' until the matter is resolved (309). At this stage, it appears that the two females will conform to stereotype and remain at home while their new husbands work to save Antonio from death.

Act 3 Scene 3

Shylock begins by telling the silent jailer to 'look' at Antonio, 'the fool that lent out money gratis' without charging interest (1, 2). The audience must feel that Antonio's predicament is unenviable and that he has been let down by Fortune and Bassanio, who is not at hand to help.

Once again, we feel Shylock is a product of a harsh society that has treated him like a 'dog' as he now warns Antonio to 'beware' his 'fangs' (6, 7).

9-1 GCSE REVISION NOTES – The Merchant of Venice

Using repetition, Shylock insists that he 'will have' his 'bond' (17). Solanio provides the biased commentary to this insistence, when he says: 'It is the most impenetrable cur/That ever kept with men' (17-18). The recurring dog imagery implies that if you treat people like animals they will behave like them, so perhaps the audience will understand Shylock's erroneous behaviour to some extent.

Act 3 Scene 4

Portia leaves Lorenzo to take control of 'the husbandry and manage' of her house in her absence as she claims that she intends 'to live in prayer and contemplation' accompanied by Nerissa (25, 28). She is conforming to the Elizabethan stereotype of women knowing their place although, of course, the reigning monarch did not conform to it herself.

Portia tells Nerissa bawdily that although they 'lack' the physical parts of men, they can more than compete 'these bragging jacks' (62, 77). This shows that despite her modesty, Portia is confident that in disguise she can match a man for ingenuity.

Act 4 Scene 1

The scene in the Duke's palace in Venice begins with the Duke describing Shylock as a 'stony adversary', which foreshadows the idea that Antonio is unlikely to receive mercy (4).

After Shylock enters the scene, the Duke mentions 'stubborn Turks' and 'Tartars', alluding to the Elizabethan perception that non-Christians are likely to show less mercy than Christians (32).

Shylock makes a strong case for not being merciful, by asking the rhetorical question: 'wouldst thou have a serpent sting thee twice?' He also reminds the audience that Christians have treated 'many a purchased slave' abjectly, purely because they feel they have ownership of another (90). He likens that to his demanding of 'the pound of flesh' from Antonio (99).

Bassanio's pleas to take his 'flesh, blood, bones, and all' instead of Antonio's falls on deaf ears, with the latter insisting that he is 'a tainted wether' or sick ram 'of the flock' (114). It seems that Bassanio, as a younger lamb of God, has more right to live his life.

Gratiano, meanwhile, mentions the Greek philosopher, 'Pythagoras', who claimed that souls could pass into another body after death (131). Gratiano suggests that Shylock's spirit is 'currish' or dog-like (133). It seems as if there can be no spiritual salvation for Shylock.

The Duke reads Bellario's letter aloud, which describes Balthazar as 'so young a body with so old a head' (160). This makes the audience and the court prepared for the disguised

9-1 GCSE REVISION NOTES – The Merchant of Venice

Portia's ingenuity.

Portia, disguised as Balthazar, makes a strong case for mercy, personalising it comparing it 'gentle rain from heaven' (181). It suggests that mercy is god-like and Shylock's lack of it implies that the Judaism is inferior to Christianity.

Shylock mistakenly considers Balthazar to be 'A Daniel come to judgement' (219). Ironically, Shylock believes that Balthazar will be like the legendary Jewish prophet, who was famous for revealing truth and promoting justice.

Fate appears to be siding with Shylock, as Antonio personifies Fortune as showing 'herself more kind/Than is her custom' (263-264). He is stoically accepting his fate, trying to convince himself that dying in this way is better than ageing without riches to comfort him.

Bassanio and Gratiano claim that Antonio's life is so valuable that their wives cannot be 'esteemed above' it (281). This creates comedy and dramatic irony for the audience know what the characters are unaware of: that their wives are witnessing their comments.

Portia's legal revelation that Shylock should 'shed no blood' in claiming his bond of a pound of flesh, prompts Gratiano to echo the Jew's words: 'I have you on the hip' (321, 330). This reminds the audience that the law is a minefield and words can be twisted to turn legal cases on their head.

Gratiano declares that Shylock should be afforded no mercy, when he says: 'A halter gratis' or a free hangman's noose should be the only mercy granted to the Jew. This seems hypocritical given how Christians are supposed to be more merciful that those of other religions.

Antonio insists that Shylock 'presently become a Christian' as part of the punishment (383). To add insult to injury, he also has to give all his possessions to 'his son Lorenzo and his daughter' once he dies (386).

Portia in disguise continues to be persuasive, saying to Bassanio that if his 'wife be not a mad woman', she would understand him giving his ring to the one who saved Antonio's life (441).

Bassanio is swayed by Portia's word and gets Gratiano to 'run and overtake' Balthazar, and give up the requested ring (448).

Act 4 Scene 2

Nerissa tries to compete with Portia, saying she'll see if she can get her 'husband's ring' (13). This makes the relationship appear a little childish.

9-1 GCSE REVISION NOTES – The Merchant of Venice

Portia brags that they'll 'outface them', which shows that she is just as guilty as men in that respect (17).

Act 5 Scene 1

Lorenzo declares that 'the moon shines bright', but then mentions some mythological ill-fated romances (1). 'Troilus' was betrayed, 'Thisbe' never met her lover, 'Dido' was deserted by her lover, as was 'Medea' (4, 8, 10, 13).

Continuing with the same theme of difficult marriages, Stephano reveals that Portia is hoping for divine intervention to save her relationship with Bassanio. She 'kneels and prays/For happy wedlock hours' (31-32).

Lorenzo, meanwhile, talks of the power of music to uplift the spirit. It seems that Jessica is unaffected by it, as she reveals: 'I am never merry when I hear sweet music' (69). It implies she lacks a soul, so even her conversion to Christianity may not save their marriage.

Nevertheless, the pair are described as 'the moon' sleeping with 'Endymion' by Portia, when she sees them together (109). Superficially, at least, they appear to be well matched.

Portia explores the double meaning of 'light', as it meant unfaithfulness as well as having its more literal meaning during Shakespeare's time (129). Again, it seems to suggest that appearances can be deceptive.

After Gratiano insultingly reveals that he gave away his 'paltry ring' (147), he adds that his 'Lord Bassanio gave his ring away' too (179). This suggests that loyalty is not something that people can rely on.

Portia's reaction is bawdy, as she insists that she will 'know' the person who took the ring (229). By that, she means she will make love with Balthazar.

Gratiano plays on the stereotypical fears of Elizabethan men when he asks a rhetorical question: 'What, are we cuckolds ere we have deserved it?' (265). Men with unfaithful wives would have been taunted or worse during that era.

The happy ending you would expect of a comedy comes to fruition as Lorenzo describes Portia's news of the inheritance that he and his wife will gain as 'manna' from heaven (293).

The play finishes on a bawdy but comedic note, as Gratiano insists that his biggest concern is 'keeping safe Nerissa's ring' (307). This suggests that the couples have been driven together on a sexual level and may not have found themselves in lasting, meaningful relationships. This may have been well received by Elizabeth I, who was never married.

9-1 GCSE REVISION NOTES – The Merchant of Venice

Sample essay question

The AQA specimen paper I'm looking at asks students to read a 24-line extract:

Signior Antonio, many a time and oft

In the Rialto you have rated me

About my monies and my usances.

Still have I borne it with a patient shrug

For suff'rance is the badge of all our tribe.

You call me misbeliever, cut-throat dog,

And spit upon my Jewish gaberdine,

And all for use of that which is mine own.

Well then, it now appears you need my help.

Go to, then, you come to me, and you say,

'Shylock, we would have monies' – you say so,

You that did void your rheum upon my beard,

And foot me as you spurn a stranger cur

Over your threshold: monies is your suit.

What should I say to you? Should I not say

'Hath a dog money? Is it possible

A cur can lend three thousand ducats?'

Or Shall I bend low, and in a bondman's key,

With bated breath and whisp'ring humbleness,

Say this: 'Fair sir, you spit on me on Wednesday last,

You spurned me such a day, another time

You called me dog: and for these courtesies

I'll lend you thus much monies.'

Students are expected to read the extract and comment about how Shakespeare presents Shylock's feelings about how is treated in the extract and elsewhere in the play.

Okay, first things first, let's look at the question. The keywords are: 'feelings' and 'treated'.

At this stage, we need to concentrate on AO2, which deals with language, form and structure. If possible we need to use literary terms to describe the language that Shakespeare uses and, of course, we need to comment on the effects. If we can do that, we can score a maximum of 12 marks for AO2. The same applies to AO1, which concerns our personal response. Finally, if we can insert some comments about context we can score a maximum of six marks for those comments.

9-1 GCSE REVISION NOTES – The Merchant of Venice

Annotated extract

Signior Antonio, many a time and oft

In the Rialto you have rated me

About my monies and my usances.

Still have I borne it with a patient shrug

For suff'rance is the badge of all our tribe.

You call me misbeliever, cut-throat dog,

And spit upon my Jewish gaberdine,

And all for use of that which is mine own.

Well then, it now appears you need my help.

Go to, then, you come to me, and you say,

'Shylock, we would have monies' – you say so,

Comment [M]: Venice's financial district

Comment [M]: Means 'insulted' here and the alliterative 'r' with Rialto makes sound like Shylock is growling like a dog, the animal he is constantly compared to

Comment [M]: Shows his fixation on all things financial.

Comment [M]: Using money to make money. As Jews were banned from many other walks of life, many had few other options than to do this.

Comment [M]: Shows that he has put up with abuse patiently, shrugging it off as if it didn't hurt him.

Comment [M]: The personification of the word 'suff'rance' and its metaphoric transformation into a badge makes the

Comment [M]: The prefix 'mis' suggests that his Jewish beliefs are wrong.

Comment [M]: Not only is he described as an animal, but more than that, Shylock has to deal with the compound adjective

Comment [M]: This distinctive, long robe would mark Shylock out as a Jew and make him an easy target for abuse.

Comment [M]: The possessive pronoun 'mine' and the word 'own' make him seem to be a greedy character, who is

Comment [M]: The word 'monies' is repeated from earlier in the speech, showing that money is an obsession for

You that did void your rheum upon my beard, | Comment [M]: Although 'void' means 'expel' here, we enter the semantic field of the law here with the word's double

And foot me as you spurn a stranger cur | Comment [M]: This graphic description of Antonio spilling watery discharge from his nose onto Shylock's beard, shows the

Over your threshold: monies is your suit. | Comment [M]: 'Foot' is a verb here, meaning 'kick'. Normally, this word would be used metaphorically, as in 'kicking

What should I say to you? Should I not say | Comment [M]: Shylock likens himself to a dog with this simile.

'Hath a dog money? Is it possible | Comment [M]: The third repetition of 'monies' as a plural shows how important money is to Shylock.

A cur can lend three thousand ducats?' | Comment [M]: The use of a rhetorical question makes Shylock appear powerful, as he is making Antonio wait upon an

Or Shall I bend low, and in a bondman's key, | Comment [M]: Another rhetorical question in quick succession makes Antonio and the audience think the

Comment [M]: The third rhetorical question mentions the sum, increasing the intensity of the effect by changing the

Comment [M]: Although there is no question mark, a fourth rhetorical question shows how ludicrous it is for the

Comment [M]: This phrase meaning a 'slave's voice' shows how demeaning life is for Shylock in Venice.

9-1 GCSE REVISION NOTES – The Merchant of Venice

With bated breath and whisp'ring humbleness,

Say this: 'Fair sir, you spit on me on Wednesday last,

You spurned me such a day, another time

You called me dog: and for these courtesies

I'll lend you thus much monies.'

Comment [M]: The alliterative 'b' emphasises how much Shylock feels he is treated little better than a slave. The metaphor 'bated breath' shows he feels he usually has to moderate his breathing in Antonio's company.

Comment [M]: The verb 'spurn' used to mean 'strike' as well as meaning to 'reject'. This adds to the impression that Shylock was physically as well as verbally abused by Antonio.

Comment [M]: Shylock uses the word 'courtesies' ironically, as he has been far from treated politely by Antonio.

Activity: Looking at my annotations and using some of your own, now try to write an essay answering the question about how Shakespeare presents 'Shylock's feelings about the way he is treated'.

Here is my response, using the DAT (Definition, Apply, Terminology) introduction plan I gave you earlier.

The phrase: 'Shylock's feelings about the way he is treated' refers to his emotional response to others in Venetian society. In the play, Christians mostly abuse Shylock, but occasionally treat him as a potentially useful pariah and, unsurprisingly, the Jew is unhappy with the treatment. Shylock meets Antonio's request for money with rhetorical questions, which makes the latter think that his 'suit' is unlikely to be successful, while reminding the Christian that his behaviour has been far from exemplary.

Shylock feels he has been demeaned by Christian society. When he mentioned how Antonio has 'railed' him in the Rialto, the alliterative 'r' makes it sound like Shylock is growling like a dog, the animal he is constantly compared to. This is an example of him behaving like a dog because he feels forced to, due to his lack of status in Venetian society. This would subtly force even a contemporary audience to reconsider how they treat people of other religions and races.

Not only is he described as an animal, but more than that, Shylock has to deal with the compound adjective 'cut-throat', which has been applied to him. Ironically, later in the play, when he demands his 'pound of flesh', he lives up to the description. However, there is no reason to believe that he committed any acts that would be considered cut-throat prior to that. We can only assume that the epithet is gained from his practice of usury, which was frowned upon by Christians, particularly.

As well as having to contend with verbal abuse, it appears from Shylock's account that he has also been physically assaulted. Shylock has been the victim of a 'Foot' attack, which means 'kick'. Normally, this word would be used metaphorically, as in 'kicking someone when they are down'. However, here it appears to accurately portray what has happened in the past, as Antonio does not interrupt in protest. It could be argued that he is simply ready to listen as his purpose is borrow money and arguments about what

9-1 GCSE REVISION NOTES – The Merchant of Venice

happened in the past may jeopardize that. Nevertheless, the arguments made against Antonio are so graphic that it is hard to imagine how he can remain silently accused if there is not a lot of truth in Shylock's accusations. The Jew uses the word 'rheum' to emphasise how Antonio expelled mucous from his nose onto Shylock's beard. Although 'void' means 'expel' here, we enter the semantic field of the law here with the word's double meaning, as contracts can be torn up as 'null and void'. In a sense, the pun 'void' foreshadows how Shylock is later tricked out of receiving his 'pound of flesh' as promised in 'the bond'. Clearly, Shylock is even unhappier at the end of the play at the perceived harsh injustice that he faces at the hands of the Christians, who insist on converting him to Christianity. Given the speculation that surrounds Shakespeare's religious views, at a time when being a Catholic could lead to dangerous accusations, it can be argued that the playwright sympathised with Shylock's situation. Despite the fact that Jews has been expelled from England, perhaps some of the contemporary audience would have also sympathised with the harsh treatment of the outsider, who feels completely alienated by society and Venice's judicial system.

Meanwhile, the depth of Shylock's feeling about the physical abuse he has suffered is revealed in the alliterative lines about 'bated breath', 'bend low' and a 'bondsman's key' The alliterative 'b' emphasises how much Shylock feels he is treated little better than a slave. The metaphor 'bated breath' shows he feels he usually has to moderate his breathing in Antonio's company, which highlights the inequalities in

Venetian society. The plosive recurring 'b' sound implies that Shylock has had to repress his emotions for so long, but now he has the upper hand on Antonio he is allowing his feelings to be expressed with this succession of 'b' words.

Finally, the use of rhetorical questions, for example: 'What should I say to you?' makes Shylock appear powerful for once and able to turn the tables on his abusers, as he is making Antonio wait upon an answer. Another rhetorical question: 'Hath a dog money?' in quick succession makes Antonio and the audience think the probable answer to the latter's 'suit' is 'no', as a dog has no 'money'. It also forces Antonio to reflect on how poorly he has treated Shylock in the past and how the Jew cannot forget the harsh treatment that has left an indelible scar on his psyche. The third rhetorical question mentions the sum 'three thousand ducats', increasing the intensity of the effect by changing the dog imagery to the more offensive word: 'cur'. Although there is no question mark, a fourth rhetorical question: 'Or shall I bend low' shows how ludicrous it is for the abused Shylock to be approached for a favour. In Venice's unequal society, the abused Shylock feels as if he is still expected to be Antonio's humble servant and pretend as if nothing has happened previously, if he must 'bend low' and give in to the latter's request.

To conclude, Shylock uses an alliterative 'r' to show how he has learned to growl like a dog, presumably due to the abuse he has received at the hands of Christians. He bears a grudge, it seems, particularly as he has been the victim of a 'foot' and 'rheum' attack. The depth of Shylock's feeling about the physical abuse he has suffered is revealed in the alliterative

9-1 GCSE REVISION NOTES – The Merchant of Venice

'b's. Rhetorical questions are arguably the most effective in revealing Shylock's emotional state, as he turns from downtrodden Jew to powerful money-lender. He seems to enjoy his moment of power, but ultimately he is destined for more 'suff'rance'.

Activity: look through the essay or your own and mark it for AO1, AO2 and AO3.

The phrase: 'Shylock's feelings about the way he is treated' refers to his emotional response to others in Venetian society. In the play, Christians mostly abuse Shylock, but occasionally treat him as a potentially useful pariah and, unsurprisingly, the Jew is unhappy with the treatment. Shylock meets Antonio's request for money with rhetorical questions, which makes the latter think that his 'suit' is unlikely to be successful, while reminding the Christian that his behaviour has been far from exemplary.

Shylock feels he has been demeaned by Christian society. When he mentioned how Antonio has 'railed' him in the Rialto, the alliterative 'r' makes it sound like Shylock is growling like a dog, the animal he is constantly compared to. This is an example of him behaving like a dog because he feels forced to, due to his lack of status in Venetian society. This would subtly force even a contemporary audience to reconsider how they treat people of other religions and races.

Not only is he described as an animal, but more than that, Shylock has to deal with the compound adjective 'cut-throat', which has been applied to him. Ironically, later in the play, when he demands his 'pound of flesh', he lives up to the description. However, there is no reason to believe that he committed any acts that would be considered cut-throat prior to that. We can only assume that the epithet is gained from his practice of usury, which was frowned upon by Christians, particularly.

As well as having to contend with verbal abuse, it appears from Shylock's account that he has also been physically assaulted. Shylock has been the victim of a 'Foot' attack, which means 'kick'. Normally, this word would be used metaphorically, as in 'kicking someone when they are down'. However, here it appears to accurately portray what has happened in the past, as Antonio does not interrupt in protest. It could be argued that he is simply ready to listen as his purpose is borrow money and arguments about what happened in the past may jeopardize that. Nevertheless, the arguments made against Antonio are so graphic that it is hard to imagine how he can remain silently accused if there is not a lot of truth in Shylock's accusations. The Jew uses the word 'rheum' to describe how Antonio expelled mucous from his nose onto Shylock's beard. Although 'void' means 'expel' here, we enter the semantic field of the law here with the word's double meaning, as contracts can be torn up as 'null and void'. In a sense, the pun 'void' foreshadows how Shylock is later tricked out of receiving his 'pound of flesh' as promised in 'the bond'. Clearly, Shylock is even unhappier at the end of the play at the perceived harsh injustice that he faces at the hands of the Christians, who insist on converting

9-1 GCSE REVISION NOTES – The Merchant of Venice

him to Christianity. Given the speculation that surrounds Shakespeare's religious views, at a time when being a Catholic could lead to dangerous accusations, it can be argued that the playwright sympathised with Shylock's situation. Despite the fact that Jews has been expelled from England, perhaps some of the contemporary audience would have also sympathised with the harsh treatment of the outsider, who feels completely alienated by society and Venice's judicial system.

Meanwhile, the depth of Shylock's feeling about the physical abuse he has suffered is revealed in the alliterative lines about 'bated breath', 'bend low' and a 'bondsman's key' The alliterative 'b' emphasises how much Shylock feels he is treated little better than a slave. The metaphor 'bated breath' shows he feels he usually has to moderate his breathing in Antonio's company, which highlights the inequalities in Venetian society. The plosive recurring 'b' sound implies that Shylock has had to repress his emotions for so long, but now he has the upper hand on Antonio he is allowing his feelings to be expressed with this succession of 'b' words.

Finally, the use of rhetorical questions, for example: 'What should I say to you?' makes Shylock appear powerful for once and able to turn the tables on his abusers, as he is making Antonio wait upon an answer. Another rhetorical question: 'Hath a dog money?' in quick succession makes Antonio and the audience think the probable answer to the latter's 'suit' is 'no', as a dog has no 'money'. It also forces Antonio to reflect on how poorly he has treated Shylock in the past and how the

Jew cannot forget the harsh treatment that has left an indelible scar on his psyche. The third rhetorical question mentions the sum 'three thousand ducats', increasing the intensity of the effect by changing the dog imagery to the more offensive word: 'cur'. Although there is no question mark, a fourth rhetorical question: 'Or shall I bend low' shows how ludicrous it is for the abused Shylock to be approached for a favour. In Venice's unequal society, the abused Shylock feels as if he is still expected to be Antonio's humble servant and pretend as if nothing has happened previously, if he must 'bend low' and give in to the latter's request.

To conclude, Shylock uses an alliterative 'r' to show how he has learned to growl like a dog, presumably due to the abuse he has received at the hands of Christians. He bears a grudge, it seems, particularly as he has been the victim of a 'foot' and 'rheum' attack. The depth of Shylock's feeling about the physical abuse he has suffered is revealed in the alliterative 'b's. Rhetorical questions are arguably the most effective in revealing Shylock's emotional state, as he turns from downtrodden Jew to powerful money-lender. He seems to enjoy his moment of power, but ultimately he is destined for more 'suff'rance'.

AO1: Personal response

AO2: The writer's effect

AO3: Context

9-1 GCSE REVISION NOTES – The Merchant of Venice

Summary of Characters

Antonio is the merchant of Venice, although Shylock is the main character in the play. He is a loyal friend to Bassanio, and literally puts his life on the line to finance the latter's pursuit of Portia. He is prepared to make the ultimate sacrifice: his life. Although modern audiences will see Antonio as a bully, his contemporaries may have viewed his treatment of Shylock as the norm. **Key quotation: 'I know not why I am so sad.' (1.1)**

Portia can be viewed as another loyal character, as she sticks to her father's plan to marry her off to the suitor who picks the lead casket. She is a powerful woman, ready to don a disguise to compete in a man's world, not unlike the reigning monarch of the time: Elizabeth I. **Key quotation: 'The quality of mercy [...] droppeth as the gentle rain from heaven' (4.1)**

Shylock is loyal to his faith, but we have to question why his daughter and servant leave his house. Nevertheless, he is a victim of abuse, who eventually attempts to bite back at his abusers. **Key quotation: 'Hath not a Jew eyes?' (3.1)**

Bassanio is loyal to Antonio, returning at his time of need. However, he is headstrong and foolish enough to give away his ring, which suggests that he will not always value his marriage with Portia. **Key quotation: 'I owe you much, and, like a willful youth,/That which I owe is lost' (1.1)**

Gratiano is a clown, so although his function in a Shakespearean play is to make light of tragic moments, he also can be relied to tell the unpalatable truth. **Key quotation: 'be thou damned, inexorable dog' (4.1)**

The same applies to **Lancelot**, the fool, who is disloyal to Shylock when he leaves his service. **Key quotation: 'Give him a present? give him a halter!' (2.2)**

Nerissa, meanwhile, is Portia's servant. She loyally follows her mistress, going in disguise to the courtroom with her. **Key quotation: 'They are as sick that surfeit with too much, as they that starve with nothing' (1.2)**

Salerio and **Solanio** are two anti-Semitic, but wealthy citizens. Their unpalatable views show how society was at the time and they narrate events, which cannot be practically portrayed on stage.

The Duke is the powerful leader of Venice, who presides over the court. He feels compelled to make sure the citizens follow the law, although he thinks Shylock is wrong not to show Antonio mercy. **Key quotation: 'We all expect a gentle answer, Jew!' (4.1)**

Jessica betrays her father and she is not seen sympathetically by many audiences as a result. The love that Lorenzo has for her may not be as genuine as it first appears, so she may also become a victim, like her father, of the unfairness present in Venetian society. **Key quotation: 'love is blind, and lovers cannot see' (2.6)**

9-1 GCSE REVISION NOTES – The Merchant of Venice

Lorenzo, her husband, has not stopped Jessica over-spending and, as already mentioned, may not love her as much as he professes. **Key quotation: 'The man that hath no music in himself […] Is fit for treasons' (5.1)**

Gobbo, Lancelot's father, is old and blind. He is employed for comic purposes, as like his son he uses numerous malapropisms.

The Prince of Morocco is like Shylock in that he seems to be a victim of prejudice. Nevertheless, he remains undaunted and has the chance to marry Portia, as long as he picks the correct casket. Ultimately, his vanity leads to him making the wrong choice. **Key quotation: 'Mislike me not for my complexion' (2.1)**

The Prince of Arragon is self-important and long-winded. It must be remembered that Elizabeth I's hated sister and previous ruler, Mary I, was the daughter of Catherine of Aragon. Contemporary audiences would have enjoyed this portrayal and the prince's ultimate failure to pick the right casket.

Essay writing tips

<u>Use a variety of connectives</u>

Have a look of this list of connectives. Which of these would you choose to use?

'ADDING' DISCOURSE MARKERS

- AND
- ALSO
- AS WELL AS
- MOREOVER
- TOO
- FURTHERMORE
- ADDITIONALLY

I hope you chose 'additionally', 'furthermore' and 'moreover'. Don't be afraid to use the lesser discourse markers, as they are also useful. Just avoid using those ones over and over again. I've seen essays from Key Stage 4 students that use the same discourse marker for the opening sentence of each paragraph! Needless to say, those essays didn't get great marks!

Okay, here are some more connectives for you to look at. Select the best ones.

9-1 GCSE REVISION NOTES – The Merchant of Venice

'SEQUENCING' DISCOURSE MARKERS

- NEXT
- FIRSTLY
- SECONDLY
- THIRDLY
- FINALLY
- MEANWHILE
- AFTER
- THEN
- SUBSEQUENTLY

This time, I hope you chose 'subsequently' and 'meanwhile'.

Here are some more connectives for you to 'grade'!

'ILLUSTRATING / EXEMPLIFYING' DISCOURSE MARKERS

- FOR EXAMPLE
- SUCH AS
- FOR INSTANCE
- IN THE CASE OF
- AS REVEALED BY

- ILLUSTRATED BY

I'd probably go for 'illustrated by' or even 'as exemplified by' (which is not in the list!). Please feel free to add your own examples to the lists. Strong connectives impress examiners. Don't forget it! That's why I want you to look at some more.

'CAUSE & EFFECT' DISCOURSE MARKERS

- BECAUSE
- SO
- THEREFORE
- THUS
- CONSEQUENTLY
- HENCE

I'm going for 'consequently' this time. How about you? What about the next batch?

'COMPARING' DISCOURSE MARKERS

- SIMILARLY
- LIKEWISE
- AS WITH
- LIKE
- EQUALLY

9-1 GCSE REVISION NOTES – The Merchant of Venice

- IN THE SAME WAY

I'd choose 'similarly' this time. Still some more to go.

'QUALIFYING' DISCOURSE MARKERS

- BUT
- HOWEVER
- WHILE
- ALTHOUGH
- UNLESS
- EXCEPT
- APART FROM
- AS LONG AS

It's 'however' for me!

'CONTRASTING' DISCOURSE MARKERS

- WHEREAS
- INSTEAD OF
- ALTERNATIVELY
- OTHERWISE
- UNLIKE

- ON THE OTHER HAND
- CONVERSELY

I'll take 'conversely' or 'alternatively' this time.

'EMPHASISING' DISCOURSE MARKERS

- ABOVE ALL
- IN PARTICULAR
- ESPECIALLY
- SIGNIFICANTLY
- INDEED
- NOTABLY

You can breathe a sigh of relief now! It's over! No more connectives. However, now I want to put our new found skills to use in our essays.

9-1 GCSE REVISION NOTES – The Merchant of Venice

Useful information/Glossary

Allegory: extended metaphor, like the grim reaper representing death, e.g. Scrooge symbolizing capitalism.

Alliteration: same consonant sound repeating, e.g. 'She sells sea shells'.

Allusion: reference to another text/person/place/event.

Ascending tricolon: sentence with three parts, each increasing in power, e.g. 'ringing, drumming, shouting'.

Aside: character speaking so some characters cannot hear what is being said. Sometimes, an aside is directly to the audience. It's a dramatic technique which reveals the character's inner thoughts and feelings.

Assonance: same vowel sounds repeating, e.g. 'Oh no, won't Joe go?'

Bathos: abrupt change from sublime to ridiculous for humorous effect.

Blank verse: lines of unrhymed iambic pentameter.

Compressed time: when the narrative is fast-forwarding through the action.

Descending tricolon: sentence with three parts, each decreasing in power, e.g. 'shouting, talking, whispering'.

Denouement: tying up loose ends, the resolution.

Diction: choice of words or vocabulary.

Didactic: used to describe literature designed to inform, instruct or pass on a moral message.

Dilated time: opposite compressed time, here the narrative is in slow motion.

Direct address: second person narrative, predominantly using the personal pronoun 'you'.

Dramatic action verb: manifests itself in physical action, e.g. I punched him in the face.

Dramatic irony: audience knows something that the character is unaware of.

Ellipsis: leaving out part of the story and allowing the reader to fill in the narrative gap.

End-stopped lines: poetic lines that end with punctuation.

Epistolary: letter or correspondence-driven narrative.

Flashback/Analepsis: going back in time to the past, interrupting the chronological sequence.

Flashforward/Prolepsis: going forward in time to the future, interrupting the chronological sequence.

Foreshadowing/Adumbrating: suggestion of plot developments that will occur later in the narrative.

9-1 GCSE REVISION NOTES – The Merchant of Venice

Gothic: another strand of Romanticism, typically with a wild setting, a sensitive heroine, an older man with a 'piercing gaze', discontinuous structure, doppelgangers, guilt and the 'unspeakable' (according to Eve Kosofsky Sedgwick).

Hamartia: character flaw, leading to that character's downfall.

Hyperbole: exaggeration for effect.

Iambic pentameter: a line of ten syllables beginning with a lighter stress alternating with a heavier stress in its perfect form, which sounds like a heartbeat. The stress falls on the even syllables, numbers: 2, 4, 6, 8 and 10, e.g. 'When now I think you can behold such sights'.

Intertextuality: links to other literary texts.

Irony: amusing or cruel reversal of expected outcome or words meaning the opposite to their literal meaning.

Metafiction/Romantic irony: self-conscious exposure of the devices used to create 'the truth' within a work of fiction.

Motif: recurring image use of language or idea that connects the narrative together and creates a theme or mood, e.g. 'green light' in *The Great Gatsby*.

Oxymoron: contradictory terms combined, e.g. deafening silence.

Pastiche: imitation of another's work.

Pathetic fallacy: a form of personification whereby inanimate objects show human attributes, e.g. 'the sea smiled benignly'. The originator of the term, John Ruskin in 1856, used 'the cruel, crawling foam', from Kingsley's *The Sands of Dee*, as an example to clarify what he meant by the 'morbid' nature of pathetic fallacy.

Personification: concrete or abstract object made human, often simply achieved by using a capital letter or a personal pronoun, e.g. 'Nature', or describing a ship as 'she'.

Pun/Double entendre: a word with a double meaning, usually employed in witty wordplay but not always.

Retrospective: account of events after they have occurred.

Romanticism: genre celebrating the power of imagination, spriritualism and nature.

Semantic/lexical field: related words about a single concept, e.g. king, queen and prince are all concerned with royalty.

Soliloquy: character thinks aloud, but is not heard by other characters (unlike in a monologue) giving the audience access to inner thoughts and feelings.

Style: choice of language, form and structure, and effects produced.

Synecdoche: one part of something referring to the whole, e.g. Carker's teeth represent him in *Dombey and Son*.

Syntax: the way words and sentences are placed together.

Tetracolon climax: sentence with four parts, culminating with the last part, e.g. 'I have nothing to offer but blood, toil, tears, and sweat ' (Winston Churchill).

ABOUT THE AUTHOR

Joe Broadfoot is a secondary school teacher of English and a soccer journalist, who also writes fiction and literary criticism. His former experiences as a DJ took him to far-flung places such as Tokyo, Kobe, Beijing, Hong Kong, Jakarta, Cairo, Dubai, Cannes, Oslo, Bergen and Bodo. He is now PGCE and CELTA-qualified with QTS, a first-class honours degree in Literature and an MA in Victorian Studies (majoring in Charles Dickens). Drama is close to his heart as he acted in Shakespeare's 'Macbeth' and 'A Midsummer Night's Dream' at the Royal Northern College of Music in Manchester. More recently, he has been teaching 'Much Ado About Nothing' to 'A' Level students at a secondary school in Buckinghamshire, 'An Inspector Calls' at a school in west London, 'Heroes' at a school in Kent and 'The Merchant of Venice' and 'The Sign of Four' at a school in south London.

Printed in Poland
by Amazon Fulfillment
Poland Sp. z o.o., Wrocław